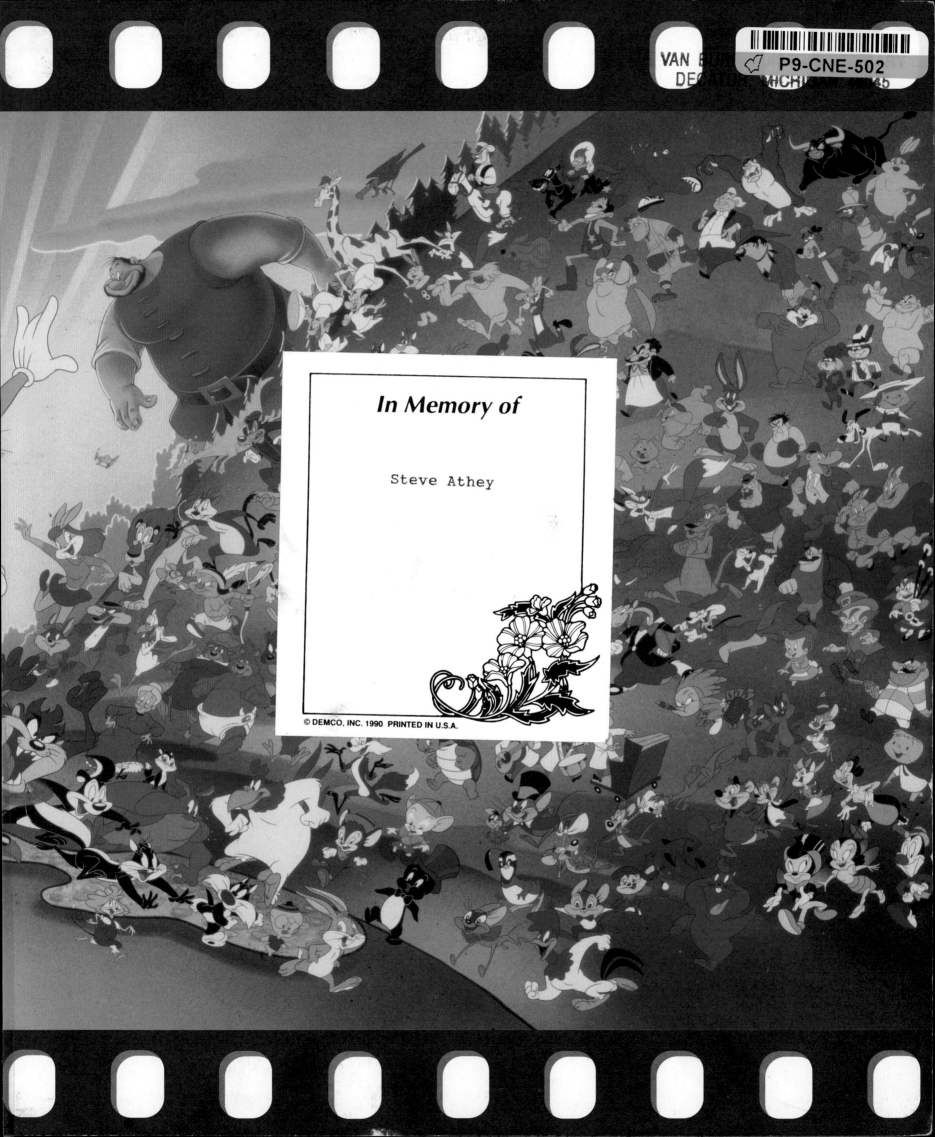

In Memory of

Steve Athey

LOONEY TUNES ™

THE ULTIMATE ~~VISUAL~~ GUIDE

Daffy

LONDON, NEW YORK, MUNICH,
MELBOURNE, and DELHI

Senior Editor Simon Beecroft
Art Editors Guy Harvey and Nick Avery
Designer Christopher Branfield
Editor Julia March
Category Publisher Alex Kirkham
Art Director Mark Richards
Publishing Manager Cynthia O'Neill Collins
Production Nicola Torode
US Editor Margaret Parrish
DTP Designer Eric Shapland

First American Edition, 2003

Published in the United States by
DK Publishing, Inc.
375 Hudson Street
New York, New York 10014

03 04 05 06 07 10 9 8 7 6 5 4 3 2 1

A Cataloging-in-Publication record for this book is available from
the Library of Congress.

ISBN 0-7894-9758-1

Reproduced by Media Development and Printing, Ltd.
Printed and bound in Italy by L.E.G.O.

Discover more at
www.dk.com

LOONEY TUNES

THE ULTIMATE VISUAL GUIDE

Jerry Beck

Tutti-fruity booby

Brazilian bombshell Carmen Miranda was caricatured in several cartoons such as *Slick Hare* and *Hollywood Canine Canteen*. In Bob Clampett's *What's Cookin' Doc?*, Bugs tries to woo the Motion Picture Academy into giving him an Oscar with his Miranda impersonation, but all he wins is the "Booby Prize Oscar."

Original animation drawing from What's Cookin' Doc?

Bugs' Granny is an effective disguise.

Wild in the country

Bugs outwits two feuding bumpkins in Robert McKimson's *Hillbilly Hare* by donning a rural "Daisy-Mae" outfit that has them going ga-ga. Bugs' square dance with brothers Curt and Pumpkinhead Martin leads to a slapstick sequence which is one of the funniest pieces of musical mayhem ever created.

Totally befuddled

Bugs employs one of his most elaborate female ensembles in Chuck Jones' *Rabbit Seasoning*. Elmer Fudd is instantly smitten and quickly seduced by Bugs' Lana Turner turn into blasting Daffy Duck once more.

The look of love!

Bugs plants a good one on the hare-baiting senator in Rebel Rabbit.

One of the boldest weapons in Bugs comic arsenal is the "wacky kiss" he plants on his foes, which usually renders them speechless. Well, what would *you* do if your enemy suddenly gave you big smack on the lips? It takes all the fight out of you, doesn't it!

HERE COMES TROUBLE

BUGS BUNNY has encountered a large share of troublemakers who never fail to underestimate his abilities. Chuck Jones established the golden rule: "Bugs must always be provoked." The rabbit never initiates conflict, but when pushed... he gives *worse* than he gets!

The Easter Rabbit

In *Easter Yeggs*, a sad-sack Easter Rabbit recruits Bugs to deliver a basket of "technicolor hen fruit" to two of his worst clients—a little brat with a hammer and Elmer Fudd trying to catch some "Easter wabbit stew." Guess which characters get egg on their faces?

Bugs is served a drugged carrot in Bewitched Bunny

Witch Hazel

This crazy cackling witch, voiced by June Foray, prides herself on her ugliness. In *Broom-Stick Bunny*, trick-or-treating Bugs challenges her supreme ugliness with his disguise. He saves Hansel and Gretel from her cooking pot in *Bewitched Bunny* and gets chased around Macbeth's castle in *A Witch's Tangled Hare*.

When Bugs hits gold ore (with his head) in *Barbary-Coast Bunny*, he is immediately suckered out of it by the villainous Nasty Canasta. Canasta uses the bunny's treasure to build a casino but, as Bugs reminds us, "You realize this is not going to go unchallenged."

Witch Hazel's haunted house

The bull was one of Bugs' fiercest opponents. Chuck Jones had no intention of making bullfighting the subject of a cartoon until the day when, out of the blue, producer Eddie Selzer instructed him not to make bullfighting films. "So I made *Bully For Bugs*," recalled Jones, "not because I was interested in bullfighting particularly, but because he said not to."

Pencil sketch of Mrs. Gorilla

Gorillas

Robert McKimson introduced Mrs. Gorilla and her henpecked husband, Gruesome, in *Gorilla My Dreams*. When Bugs agrees to be their child, Gruesome is less than thrilled. Papa gorilla ends up knocking himself out by chasing "junior" through the jungle. He gets another pounding in the follow-up, *Apes of Wrath*.

"Don't they look yummy-yummy?"

"Whomp your partner with all your might...."

Double trouble

When Bugs sees double, he knows it's trouble. Curt and Pumpkinhead Martin are a pair of twisted mountain men in *Hillbilly Hare*. The wabbit outsmarts the pair by calling a hilarious square dance, forcing them to pull beards, whomp each other with fence posts and wallow in the pig pen.

Witch Hazel has always had a thing for Bugs Bunny. "You look like Paul—my pet tarantula," she pines.

What's cooking?

In *French Rarebit*, set in Paris, twin chefs Francois and Louie fight over the bunny's secret recipe for "Louisiana Bayou Backbay Bunny Borderlay, à la Antoine." This requires both cooks to become stand-in rabbits and be broiled in oil. *C'est magnifique!*

In *Hyde and Hare*, Bugs convinces Dr. Jekyll to adopt him—not realizing he has a little secret....

Nero Lion receives a lesson in circus etiquette from Bugs in *Acrobatty Bunny*.

Bugs convinces the Snowman that Daffy Duck is *The Abominable Snow Rabbit*.

A Mohican aims to give Bugs a "hare cut and scalp treatment" in *A Feather In His Hare*.

The Big Bad Wolf tries to outsmart Bugs in *Now, Hare This* and *False Hare*.

Here's where this book *really* begins!

TRULY DAFFY

DAFFY DUCK was the first character to truly personify Warner Bros.' madcap humor. In his early cartoons, he is totally deranged: bouncing off the walls, singing "Merry-Go-Round Broke Down" (the Looney Tunes title music), and driving Hollywood directors crazy—silly, surreal, and hilarious. Altogether now: "Woo-hoo-hoo!"

Daffy stole the show in Tex Avery's cartoon, Porky's Duck Hunt.

"¡OOH ¡OOM"

First appearance

Daffy began life as what Chuck Jones called a "wild and unrestrained screwy duck." In *Porky's Duck Hunt*, Daffy bounces across a marsh, laughing hysterically at the pudgy pig and his dog (here named Rin-Tin-Tin) until the frustrated pig points out a move that isn't in the script. The duck simply replies, "I'm just a crazy darn-fool duck." And how!

Original pencil animation from Porky's Duck Hunt

Daffy and Porky appear on an animator's model sheet.

True original

Daffy Duck was the first cartoon character to be named after a state of utter lunacy, predating "Bugs" Bunny and the "Goofy" Gophers. Daffy was also unique in that he had no reason to be so manic—he just was! Each director found ways to develop the duck's character, adding something new to the mix and making him increasingly complex.

Big star

Daffy's rise to stardom was meteoric. "People weren't accustomed to seeing a cartoon character do these things," said director Bob Clampett. "People would leave the theaters talking about this daffy duck."

This is what happens when you get stuck in an artificial lung.

Porky's pal

In his early pairings with Porky, Daffy played the clown to the stuttering pig's straight man. In *Porky And Daffy* (right) the pig assists as the slap-happy duck's boxing manager. As *The Daffy Doc* (above), the duck plucks a perfectly healthy Porky off the street and chases him around a madcap medical center. They end up falling through an artificial lung, which causes each of their body parts to inflate in turn.

Aspiring star Daffy won't let movie producer I.M. Stupendous say no *in* Daffy Duck In Hollywood.

Two nuts together

Daffy's appearance in *Daffy Duck And Egghead* is his all-time craziest. In the opening titles, two "nuts" emerge from walnut shells—Daffy and Egghead, the human hunter who will become Elmer Fudd. Director Tex Avery gives the hunter a classic gag that breaks the fourth wall: Egghead shoots a guy in the audience who won't sit down! At the end, the men (actually, the ducks) in the white coats take Daffy away.

In Robert McKimson's *Daffy Doodles*, Daffy plays the part of the "mustache maniac." He paints mustaches on billboards, subway riders, and irate policemen (including Porky) all over the city. Then, when he is taken to court, he is found "not guilty"—by a mustachioed jury!

Dr. I.C. Spots: CASE NOTES
DAFFY DUCK

As you will see on the next few pages, Mr. Daffy Duck is one of the strangest cases of split personality I have ever encountered. He evolved from one neurosis to another—from a raving lunatic to a selfish, egotistical scoundrel, with delusions of grandeur. I have monitored his actions very closely and I'm sure you will agree: This one's for the birds!

Henpecked quack

The flip side to Daffy's lunacy is his role as a troubled married man and father. In *The Henpecked Duck* (right), Daffy's wife wants to divorce him for losing her eggs while practicing a magic disappearing trick.

Daffy the inebriated daddy duck in Wise Quacks

Cross-eyed and madcap!

Daffy traits

Jumping, spinning, and shouting "woo-hoo-hoo"—these are the trademarks of the early, Looney Tuney Daffy Duck. Other common traits include a cross-eyed glaze, gobs of spit emitted when talking, and offering to read the bumps on people's heads (after creating the bumps first).

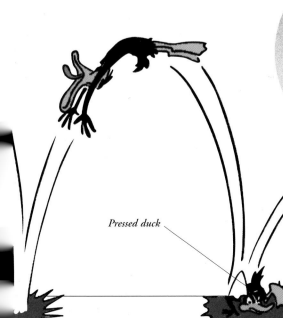

Pressed duck

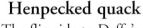

Scenic settings

Part of the charm of Speedy's cartoons lies in the stylized art of Mexican rural locales. This layout drawing of a village square, by Hawley Pratt (right), featured in *Gonzales Tamales*.

"ARRIBA! ARRIBA!"

Speedy's slow pal

Speedy's cousin, Slowpoke Rodriguez, makes up for his lack of pace in *Mexicali Schmoes* and *Mexican Boarders* with his gunfighting and hypnotism skills.

"MEXiCAN BOARDERS"
a LOONEY TUNE CARTOON
TECHNICOLOR®

WARNER BROS. CARTOON

Mexican cats

Speedy is a legend throughout Mexico. But fame has a price—he is often pursued by cats who want the glory of catching the famous rodent. In the Oscar-nominated *Mexicali Shmoes*, directed by Friz Freleng, fat Jose and skinny Manuel try (and fail) to make a meal of Speedy.

Catch him if you can, Pussy-gatos!

In *Tabasco Road*, Speedy speedily substitutes a stick of dynamite in a cat's mouth for his friend Pablo!

DAZZLING DAMES

The Barnyard Dawg doubles as the Fudds' "Wover."

THE LOONEY TUNES appear to be a mostly male menagerie, but don't be fooled. They've got distaff star power too, and the Warner Bros. girls are one striking, saucy, and seriously screwball sorority. Young and old, sweet and sour, from dreamers to schemers to eating machines—all the female charmers are right here.

The world's worst wabbit hunter has at weast been wucky in womance. Elmer Fudd's equally dim, equally language-warping significant other helped her hubby face off with Daffy in *Don't Axe Me*.

Granny plays as hard as the rest!

Lola Bunny—Baseball pro... and a babe to boot

Spin sister

She might wear lipstick, a bow, and high heels but She-Devil is no fragile fashion victim. After Bugs marries her to Taz on-screen in *Devil May Hare*, the down-under wonder girl proceeds to snarl and spin as hungrily as her beau. She swings a mean rolling pin, too—effective in *Bedevilled Rabbit* when cross-dressed Bugs intrudes on her territory.

Chat room

Minding her own business in France, Penelope the Cat always manages to get a white stripe painted down her back. That's when skunk lover Pepe Le Pew arrives on the scene, pursuing the feline in hope of a stinky soiree.

Double dribble

The Tune Squad prove basketball amateurs in *Space Jam* until Lola Bunny arrives to show off a few moves... and curves. With her Bugs-enticing catch phrase "Don't call me doll!", Lola moved on from the feature film to become a recurring pizza delivery girl in the comics.

Mini-meow

Tiny Pussyfoot can melt the hardest heart, reducing bulldog Marc Antony to big-brotherly mush in Chuck Jones' classics *Feed the Kitty* and *Cat Feud*.

Field of operations

A sophisticated hunter works with every element of the landscape. In this desert terrain, ledges make handy spying points and excellent launch sites for missiles, while crevasses provide ready-made pitfalls, and basins are perfect spots from which to fire rockets upward. The only trouble with the desert is that its advantages can become disadvantages when your prey is unwilling to accept that you are a supergenius.

Hazards

If a truck hits a coyote in the desert and nobody notices, has he really been clobbered? The answer is yes—motor vehicles forever ambush Wile E. at the most uncomfortable times, and with the most deceptively Road Runner-like sounds. Beep-beep!

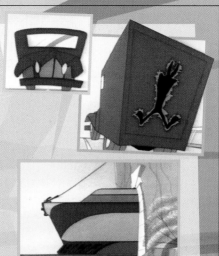

The common locomotive is big trouble for the Coyote. They don't just hit him—they carry him miles away from the Road Runner.

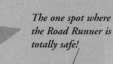

The one spot where the Road Runner is totally safe!

Acme cannon: ready, aim, backfire.

Acme grease: to send you down the slippery slope

Dead-end bridge: for chasing your prey over the edge

High bridge: good for looking down on lesser creatures

Painted truck tunnel: beware of beep-beeping!

Wile E. mines his own business.

Birdseed: tempting, aromatic, boobytrapped

Unlit mine shaft: strike match, find TNT stockade.

Bugs' desert home: Albuquerque, New Mexico

Three-wheel rocket: when two wheels just aren't enough

The painted desert

Parts of this prairie don't really exist—or do they? Artist as well as predator, Wile E. makes landscape paintings to disguise Road Runner-trapping cliffs and dead ends. But the images turn frustratingly real—and artificial once again—usually whenever it's least convenient for the Coyote.

UNFORGETTABLE

WARNER BROS. had a genius for creating
memorable cartoon characters. Even those who
appeared in just one film or a handful of cartoons made
an unforgettable mark on our consciousness. They are
the beloved supporting stars: the gangsters, gremlins,
singing frogs, mice, penguins, and daydreamers.
What would Looney Tunes be without them?

SHOW STOPPERS

WE OFTEN THINK of the Looney Tunes gang as performers—they have all the skills of a great repertory company: snappy slapstick, manic melodrama, and vicious verbal gags. Two characters, however, stand out from the others as genuine stage performers. Enter singing, dancing Michigan J. Frog and baby mime Playboy Penguin.

Going for croak

In the Chuck Jones masterpiece, *One Froggy Evening*, a member of a wrecking crew looks inside the cornerstone of a demolished building and finds a frog in a box. Michigan J. Frog, released from his 50 years' entombment, demonstrates a most unfroglike ability to sing and dance.

Do the Michigan

Michigan J. Frog's music repertoire features 1890s hits such as "Hello Ma Baby," "I'm Just Wild About Harry," and "Please Don't Talk About Me When I'm Gone." One song, "The Michigan Rag," was a faux-Nineties riff specially created for the cartoon.

"I'M JUST WILD ABOUT HARRY"

The box contains the cornerstone document along with the frog.

Trying to induce an encore. Flabby, ain't he? *Ribbit!*

Torpid toad

Alas, after his exuberant songs and dances, the frog reverts to lazy froghood. His new owner, dreaming of big money, considers this no big deal—at least at first.

Voice of the frog

Singer, actor, and bandleader Bill Roberts was the singing voice for Michigan J. Frog in *One Froggy Evening*. Roberts' baritone voice was frequently heard in films such as *The Greatest Show On Earth* and he performed in small parts while under contract to MGM. According to studio records, when he recorded his tracks for Chuck Jones, the film was originally titled *It Hopped One Night*.

These humanlike arms turn into froggy flippers when the show is over.

Frog flop

In one theater after another, the fates conspire to prevent anyone other than Michigan's owner from seeing him in action. Finally, the now-destitute owner reburies the frog—for another would-be moneymaker (or T.V. network) to rediscover years later.

94

Little bird lost

When pantomime ice-skater Playboy Penguin gets lost in Brooklyn in *8-Ball Bunny*, Bugs offers to take him home. The continent-hopping trip is fraught with dangers including a hungry hobo who thinks "penguins is practically chickens!" At last, Bugs gets Playboy to the South Pole—only to find out that the penguin was really born in Hoboken, New Jersey.

Antarctic antics

In *Frigid Hare*, directed by Chuck Jones, the little penguin is a genuine South Pole dweller, with Bugs as an accidental tourist (after taking a wrong turn at Albuquerque). Reluctantly hanging around to babysit the silent bird, Bugs winds up protecting him from an uninvited third party.

A top hat six inches tall sounds small—but not if you're a penguin 10 inches tall.

Playboy's southern transportation in *8-Ball Bunny* includes the steamship S. S. Admiral Byrd. There, Bugs finds the star performer debuting on the ship's menu.

Bugs turns royal performer in the Oscar-winning *Knighty Knight Bugs*—but a king's order transforms him from jester to jouster.

Giovanni dances to his own tune (above) until the wabbit tricks him into holding a high note until his face turns green (right).

Giovanni Jones

In *Long Haired Hare*, Bugs Bunny's banjo, harp, and tuba playing disturb the precious eardrums of Giovanni Jones, opera singer. When the baritone batters the bunny allegro, our rabbit replies, "Of course you know this means war!" and a musical melee breaks out on stage.

In *Big Top Bunny*, Bugs is challenged by the jealous Bruno The Magnificent, the egotistical star of Colonel Corny's World Famous Circus. After being tricked on the trapeze act, the bunny gets even by blasting Bruno from a cannon.

Bugs tricks Bruno into taking a high dive from 5000 feet into a block of fresh cement.

Maurice Noble produced this concept painting for Zoom And Bored.

Noble's stylized jungle featured in Boyhood Daze.

Keeping it unreal

Over time, Warner Bros. animations began to feature sparser, less realistic background settings. Surreal space landscapes by Maurice Noble, abstract Tasmanian jungles by Richard H. Thomas, and simple Mexican mouse traps by Tom O'Loughlin were stylish and contemporary.

Rocket Squad featured layouts by Ernie Nordli and background art by Philip De Guard.

Heroic design

Each cartoon demanded between 30 and 50 backgrounds, which had to be produced at great speed. Background artists are the true heroes of animated cartoons. Richard H. Thomas, Paul Julian, Irv Wyner, Tom O'Loughlin, and Philip De Guard (right) are among Warners' best.

Philip De Guard adopts a more abstract style in Bewitched Bunny.

Paul Julian painted this nautical background for Mutiny On The Bunny.

A dynamite Richard H. Thomas set from The Oily American.

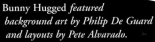

Bunny Hugged featured background art by Philip De Guard and layouts by Pete Alvarado.

"Talking" books

Capitol Records contracted with Mel Blanc to appear in an audio series originally sold as 78 rpm vinyl records. The albums were accompanied by story books illustrated by either Robert, Tom, or Charles McKimson.

Bugs Bunny (above) featured three stories: "Bugs Bunny Meets Elmer Fudd," "Porky Pig In Africa," and "Daffy Duck Flies South."

The story features Cecil Tortoise from Tortoise Beats Hare.

Activity books

Cutout books, sticker albums, connect-the-dots, paper dolls, and other activity books are a staple at drug and toy stores. These two were published by Whitman, a subsidiary of Western Publishing Co.

Premiums and giveaways

Special publications were created for promotional purposes. Looney Tunes character comics were included in packages of Cheerios cereal, Quaker Oats Puffed Rice, and Kool Aid. Special issues of March Of Comics featuring Bugs or Porky were distributed at Sears department stores.

Books and comics often feature Looney Tunes characters in very different guises to the cartoon films.

Comic differences

The original comic-book personas for the Looney Tunes characters sometimes differed in print from the animated films. Road Runner, for example, spoke and ran through the desert with his three nephews in the comics, while Sniffles the Mouse was teamed with a little girl named Mary Jane, who had magic powers.

Western Publishing created hundreds of children's comic books.

War Bonds provided extra revenue for the war effort.

BACK IN ACTION 1

IN THEIR BIGGEST feature film yet, Bugs Bunny and Daffy Duck co-star with actors Brendan Fraser, Jenna Elfman, and Steve Martin in *Looney Tunes: Back In Action*. Blockbuster action combines with spectacular animation and a hilarious story which, like the classic shorts, breaks the fourth wall and runs off in surprising directions—all strictly for laughs!

The plot

When Daffy Duck and security guard D.J. Drake (Fraser) are fired from Warner Bros., Bugs Bunny and Vice President of Comedy Kate (Elfman) follow them. The four set off to rescue Drake's missing father—action star Damian Drake (Timothy Dalton), who is really a spy being hunted by the chairman of the Acme Corporation (Martin).

The story starts on the actual Warner Bros. backlot in Burbank, California.

Damian's Drake's rocket-powered spy car is filled with cool gadgets.

An all-star cast

Timothy Dalton, Heather Locklear, pro-wrestler Bill Goldberg, and NASCAR's champion racer Jeff Gordon provide co-starring roles and cameo appearances. Looney Tunes appearing in the film include Tweety, Wile E. Coyote, Marvin The Martian, Granny, and many others.

Joe Dante

Director Joe Dante directed *Gremlins*, *Small Soldiers*, and *The Howling*, but the Looney Tunes proved his greatest challenge. Bugs was the hardest of all: "Because of his persona, the fact that he has to remain cool at all times and always be on top of everything," Dante recalls. "Daffy is much more malleable because he's crazy and has neuroses."

The movie includes scenes inside Yosemite Sam's casino.

Watch out for in-jokes in the casino, including a photo of Chuck Jones!

Eric Goldberg

Animation Supervisor Eric Goldberg is a veteran Disney animator who co-directed the features *Pocahontas* and *Fantasia 2000* and created the animation of the genie in *Aladdin*. His career has been influenced by his personal friendships with Looney Tunes luminaries Chuck Jones, animator Ken Harris, and layout artist Maurice Noble.

Bugs and Daffy

Eric Goldberg thinks Bugs is the greatest animation character ever, but he admits that this is Daffy's movie. "He steals every scene he's in," says Goldberg. "And after all those years of being a second banana, I think he deserves it!"

The movie stays true to the classic personas of the Looney Tunes.

133

BACK IN ACTION 2

TO MAKE THE MOVIE, a new world had to be created—a place where cartoons and people "don't discriminate against each other, don't act surprised when a talking duck walks into a room," as director Joe Dante explains. Of course, the world of *Looney Tunes: Back In Action* also had to be designed and built by talented craftsmen at Warner Bros. in Hollywood.

Acme headquarters

The power-hungry Acme Corporation is the setting where Mr. Chairman (Steve Martin) plots to rule the world—once he can snatch the fabled Blue Monkey diamond from Daffy, Bugs, and D.J. Drake. "Steve Martin ad libbed 90 percent of his part and created a character that wasn't in the script," says director Dante. "Steve made him a wonderfully crazy Looney Tune kind of a guy."

The Acme chairman plans to use the diamond's power to superevolve the company, giving it "an unbeatable edge in a tight marketplace"!

Paris

One of the most memorable animation sequences in the film is Bugs', Daffy's, and Elmer's chase through the Louvre art museum in Paris. They jump in and out of various famous paintings and take on the style of each one, melting in the Dali and becoming pointillist in the Seurat.

A preproduction drawing depicts Paris.

Los Angeles Exposition Park stood in for Paris in some scenes.

Production designer Bill Brzeski gave Acme's monolithic headquarters a retro-futuristic look.

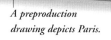

When in France, do as Pepe Le Pew does.